N

Moppa

Kalimna

Greenock

Nuriootpa

Barossa
Bushgardens

Marananga

Angaston

Moculta

Ranges

Tanunda

Keyneton

Tanunda Ck

Bethany

1

Barossa

North Para River

Jacob's Creek

5

4

Lyndoch

Eden Valley

South Para River

3

Para
Wirra
Recreation
Park

Williamstown

Boehm Springs
Reserve

2

Springton

6

Mt Crawford
Forest

Greenock Ck

Du...us Ck

GW01252162

This edition of Wild Barossa is proudly sponsored by:

Wild Barossa

"how plants, people & wildlife connect."

for Carolyn

"A thing is right when it tends to preserve the integrity, stability, and beauty of the biotic community. It is wrong when it tends otherwise."

"When we see land as a community to which we belong, we may begin to use it with love and respect."

Aldo Leopold (1887-1948)

Chris Hall

First published by Openbook Howden Print & Design for C M Hall, PO Box 565 TANUNDA SA 5352

© Chris Hall 2016

Author: Hall, Chris.

Title: Wild Barossa: how plants, people & wildlife connect

ISBN: 978-0-9946139-0-5 (softcover)

Notes: Includes map, contributors' page, bibliography, endnotes, photo credits and wildlife index.

Subjects: flora and fauna of the Barossa Valley, South Australia; wildlife stories.

Proudly designed and printed in South Australia.

Graphic design: Avylon Magarey

Photographic editor: Guy Draper

Printing and Binding: Openbook Howden Print and Design, www.openbookhowden.com.au

For further copies of this book contact Chris Hall
chall.tanunda@gmail.com

website://http:wildbarossa.com.au

Printed by Openbook Howden
using Forest Stewardship Council®
certified paper and vegetable based inks.

Contents

Foreword: how plants, people & wildlife connect

Heading east along Gomersal Rd towards Tanunda I breathe a sigh of relief: the city lies behind me and I see the Barossa Ranges beckoning. Unique. So what is the attraction, what is so good about being in the Barossa?

The sense of place is defined in part by a region's local plants and wildlife. Whilst 'terroir' connects the quality of the soil and sense of place, a fuller expression of connectivity to place must surely extend to its flora and fauna. Wildlife is one of the Barossa's treasures, to be celebrated for its own sake, as well as adding to our quality of life. Then it struck me that no one had yet written a book twinning the local flora and fauna and showing how they interact and depend upon each other, so this is such a book. The book then goes one step further, in joining the dots between wildlife, plants and agriculture.

Think of the Barossa as a vast naturepark, not just a wine region. It is a haven for wildlife, and much of it exists in vineyard rows and backyards. What I find exciting and what the book has tapped into is the community and industry trend of embracing the co-existence of wildlife and agriculture. There is an emerging consciousness about these connections which weave us all into a common landscape.

Wild Barossa is 'a people book' full of wildlife stories. Over a hundred mainly local people have contributed to it and I feel like the conduit who has quietly gathered and distilled their stories.

Three themes are woven through the book:

- how people are working *with* Nature in the Barossa
- how Nature is adopting and adapting to viticulture, naturally
- the concept of connectivity

It is useful to ask the question: how does a plant (gum tree, wattle, flower) need an animal/bird/bug and conversely, how does the fauna need the plant? The example of the increasing numbers of White-winged Choughs in the Barossa illustrates all three themes: how do they need the vineyard and how does the vineyard need them? Winery-hopping choughs scratch away at the straw mulch and despatch earwigs, hence it's a win/win: the choughs get a tasty meal and a vineyard pest is kept in check. And here's the thing: the choughs are not only tolerated but encouraged by the locals, as they move seamlessly from adjacent woodland to and from the vineyard.

Wild Barossa champions one other new concept: 'leaflife'. I always resented the negative connotations of 'leaf litter' as something to be thrown away, as waste. There is 'wildlife', 'birdlife' and so now there is 'leaflife'. Leaflife should be appreciated and encouraged, as a natural process which helps sustain our soils, our plants and our wildlife.

Finally, profiling nine local heroes in the book further underlines how viticulture and the community are working actively *with* Nature for mutually beneficial outcomes: these are people with passion who understand why Nature matters.

Sincere thanks to all the people whose local knowledge, insights and stories helped make this book possible.

Luke Allen
James Altmann
Jan Angas
Alison Annells
Roy Baier
Terri Bateman
Neville Bonney
Barossa Bushgardens
Veronica Clayton
Megan Coles
Di Davidson
Mark Douglas
Ray Duance
James Ehrat
Carolyn Evitts
Daniel Falkenberg
Ian Falkenberg
Steve Fiebiger
Jan Forrest/SA Museum
Ingrid Glastonbury
Jeremy Gramp
Yvonne Gravier
Marie Hage
Valmai Hall
Kerry Hayden
Don Helbig
Prue Henschke
Angela Heuzenroeder
Dr Katja Hogendoorn/Uni of
    Adelaide

Dr Philippa Horton/SA Museum
Brooke Howell
Shawn Kalleske
Greg & Sam Kretschmer
Tammy Leggett
Margaret Lehmann
Mike Leske
Jeff Liersch
Kerstin Lohmeyer
Fiona MacLachlan
Dr Mike McKelvey
Bob Myers
Ngadjuri Nations Aboriginal
    Corporation
Amanda Pearce
Grant Penrhyn
Topa Petit/Uni SA
Sally & Martin Pfeiffer
Cathy Potts
Graham Powell
Luke Price
Mike Quarmby
RDA Barossa
Mary Retallack
Bev Rice
Susanne Richards
Dr Peggy Rismiller
Nicki Robins
Peter Robinson
Dr Phillip Roetman/Uni SA

Tim Scheiner
Jacky Schutz
Kerry Schwier
Jo Seabrook
Adrian Shackley
James Smith/FauNature
Kim Smith
John Stafford
David Stammer/SA Museum
Chris Steeles
Steve Taylor
Jamie Turley
Sue Vogt
Trevor Waldhuter
Steve Walker
Peter Wall
Jason van Weenen
Necia, Frank & Juliette Wilden
Glenys Wood
Dr Maryam Yazdani/Uni of
    Adelaide
Feng Yi

Graphic design Avylon Magarey
Photographic editor Guy Draper

Rough-barked Manna Gum
Eucalyptus viminalis subspecies *cygnetensis*

Habitat hotel

Sought-after accommodation and larder for all manner of woodland wildlife. Hospitable hollows and layers of chunky bark strips form a haven of hidey-holes which are insect hotels and this is why insects, spiders, bugs and birds all call manna gums home.

Flora for fauna

This tree is loved by koalas, both the White-throated and Brown Treecreepers and other woodland birds such as blue wrens and honeyeaters. It also provides tree hollows for kookaburras, and is a happy hunting ground for echidnas foraging in the leaflife and fallen logs at its base. Its branches and hollows are generally booked out months in advance.

Best on show
- Barossa Ranges: along Tanunda Creek Rd
- Boehm Springs Reserve
- Heggies Range Rd
- Kaiser Stuhl Conservation Park

It took this kookaburra and its mate three months to eject a family of possums from this five-star tree hollow. The strategy of repeatedly dive-bombing the hollow, then hammering and tapping at the door with their beaks eventually proved too much for the possums, who raised the white flag of surrender and moved out in disgust! The persistent kookaburras moved right in to breed, taking some three months before junior flew out of his hollow into the world.

A gravity-defying White-naped Honeyeater gleaning insects from the bark.

Experience the magic, power and eerie presence of this ancient tree at Boehm Springs Reserve, near Springton. Timeless.

Right: Koalas are increasingly calling the Barossa home, in a natural expansion of their range northwards from the Adelaide Hills. Rough-barked Manna Gum is one of their feeding trees. They also eat red gum and stringybark as well as other gums.

Peppermint Box
Eucalyptus odorata

Capturing the local spirit of place

The local Ngadjuri people closely identify with this tree, and were called the "Peppermint Gum people" by neighbouring tribes.[1] The geographic range of the Peppermint Box from Nuriootpa northwards falls within part of the Ngadjuri's traditional area.

Flora for fauna

Habitat heaven. Gums older than one hundred years provide tree hollows for nesting birds, bats, possums and bees. Branches are critical habitat and perches for threatened woodland birds such as robins, Owlet-nightjars, Grey Shrikethrush, honeyeaters and so on. Eucalypts generate huge quantities of leaflife, providing ground layer habitat for echidnas, skinks and many smaller bugs, insects and critters.

Vital statistics

- Small to medium tree, 5-10m tall, with a spreading habit; may be multi-stemmed
- Prefers clay soils, sandy loam to clay loam
- Rough brown to grey bark on trunk, pale and smooth on upper limbs

White to cream flowers autumn-spring, in bundles.

Best on show

- Whistler Wines, Marananga
- isolated paddock gums on Valley floor, Moppa and Marananga.
- on gentle slopes in the Barossa Ranges. Elsewhere on rocky slopes and ridges

Right: echidnas need habitat provided by large gums such as fallen logs.

Shawn Kalleske from Moppa typifies the viticulturists who actively foster beneficial wildlife connections in vineyards.

Old Peppermint Box gums like this one on Hutton Vale Farm are increasingly being protected and recognised for their habitat value.

Tawny Frogmouth, the master of disguise, pretending not to be seen.

Owlet-nightjars nest in tree hollows provided by old gums.

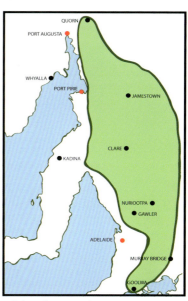

Local distribution of Peppermint Box.

4

River Red Gum
Eucalyptus camaldulensis subspecies *camaldulensis*

Where eagles dare

Penthouse privacy is assured thirty metres up a gum tree. The Barossa's biggest gums provide prime nesting sites for large birds of prey as well as being homes, beds and supermarkets for other wildlife.

Flora for fauna

There are seven known nesting sites for Wedge-tailed Eagles in the Barossa (refer inside cover map), often in red gums near watercourses or in blue gums and Peppermint Box.[2] Most eagle territories have several nests but one is favoured for breeding. There are reports of nests being used for well over a century. Eagles failed to breed when rabbits were in very low numbers.[3] As well as providing nesting sites for large raptors, demand for tree hollows in large gums outstrips supply. Galahs, kookaburras, owls, possums, bats, bees all need tree hollows for breeding.

Vital statistics
• grows typically on river flats and along creekbeds that receive seasonal flooding

That eyrie feeling: flying practice for a young Wedge-tailed Eagle about to leave the nest high up in a red gum.

Best on show
• Jacob's Creek Visitor Centre
• Barossa Bushgardens
• Seppeltsfield Winery creekline
• paddock trees around Eden Valley

Tree hollows take 90-120 years to form. Red gums can live up to 600 years.

Nankeen Kestrel with a mouse. Birds of prey need tall trees.

Adept at adapting: Galah numbers have grown since European settlement.

A red gum's welcome presence in the distance often signifies the existence of a watercourse. This tree, 'The Old Gum Tree' on the river floodplain at Barossa Bushgardens, has had its original understorey species replanted to assist tree health. Little Falcons and Nankeen Kestrels have bred in The Old Gum Tree in recent times. It is common for a pair of Little Falcons to hunt together, with one falcon flushing birds from cover and acting as a distraction, whilst the second one waits out of view ready to swoop on the prey.

Soaring Wedge-tailed Eagle (right). They are easily identified in flight by their upswept wings.
Southern Boobook: an owl's haunting call of 'mopoke, mopoke' is a welcome sound at night, breaking the stillness in Barossa towns (far right).

Drooping Sheoak
Allocasuarina verticillata

A complex diamond

Multi-faceted. She is the Jessica Watson of Barossa flora: can be a solo voyager, seen gracing a distant rocky ridgeline; but equally at home as an understorey tree that knows her place as a team player nestled beneath the taller woodland gums.
The Drooping Sheoak will be voted Tree of the Year in 2500 because she's as tough as diamonds, loves a good drought, and is prone to hedonistic sunbaking.

Flora for fauna
This tree is for the birds! Rare Glossy Black Cockatoos on Kangaroo Island avoid extinction by eating the seed within the woody seed cones on the female tree. In the Barossa it tends to be Adelaide Rosellas, Beautiful Firetails and other finches, silvereyes and thornbills that adore its winged seeds, and it forms a small part of Yellow-tailed Black Cockatoos' diet.[4] Diamond Firetails build their grassy nests high in the crown of sheoaks.

Let the children play
- cones are great 'loose parts' to play with and create crafts
- doesn't drop large branches, a safer tree to plant around children

Yellow-rumped Thornbill.

Striated Thornbill. Several species of thornbill love flitting through the canopy in search of insects and seeds.

Seed cones: only the female tree has the cones. Children love playing with them.

Best on show
- Barossa Bushgardens
- Menglers Hill Lookout
- Barossa Ranges road verges
- Moppa Hill

Design me!
- The accumulation of needles over time creates a weed-free space beneath the tree with the build-up of leaflife. This takes 4-5 years

Adelaide Rosellas feed on sheoak seeds extracted from the woody cones.

Rest or camp beneath a sheoak to appreciate the soughing of the wind through the needles.

Giant ancient Drooping Sheoak in Boehm Springs Reserve.

Zebra Finch: various finches are attracted to sheoaks for the tiny winged seeds which they glean from the woody seed cones.

South Australian Inland Blue Gum
Eucalyptus leucoxylon subspecies *pruinosa*

Big blond Barossa businessman

Success sits easily on this blond-barked local's branches. His main business, nectar production, is blooming. In addition he juggles a diverse portfolio of ethical investments – wildlife, birdlife, and leaflife. Definitely makes the Barossa 'A List.'

Flora for fauna

Crested Shriketits frequent blue gums to strip the decorticating bark in search of insects. Cream flowers are a nectar source for honeyeaters, lorikeets, insects, bees. Tree hollows in large trees are habitat and nesting niches for birds, possums, bees. Fallen leaflife and branches are habitat for many creatures such as skinks and geckos.

Marbled Gecko. Eucalypts produce leaflife (leaf litter), which is habitat.

Vital statistics

- blue gums produce the most nectar of any flowering native - a massive 1400 kilojoules per day[5]
- grows to 20 metres, commonly seen in paddocks
- cream flowers, smooth bark
- distinctive gumnuts are the shape of a rounded wine glass, much larger than many other local gumnuts

Crested Shriketits adore something about blue gums - the special insects they expose and glean from peeling off the bark.

Best on show

- Nuriootpa High School Blue Gum woodland in town's main street
- Jack Bobridge Cycle Track, Nuriootpa-Angaston section
- Barossa Bushgardens
- Gnadenberg Rd, eastern end

Rare blue gum woodland in Nuriootpa's main street in the grounds of Nuriootpa High School. Echidnas and kangaroos are still sighted here probably because of its proximity to the river which is a natural wildlife corridor.

Pardalotes are Nature's gold, tiny and precious, as they clip off the lerp insects from gum leaves, thereby keeping the foliage healthy. Plus they have a delightful call resonating across the woodland treetops– a high-pitched "chip-chip" with the accent on the second syllable.

Don Helbig is a fifth generation local and self-taught naturalist. As a boy on the family farm, before the first tractor and with domestic power supplied only from the 32 volt petrol-powered milking machine, he recalls it was almost unheard of to see a kangaroo in the Barossa. Don's boyhood had known the glory of bushland alive with orchids, lilies and wildlife, and learned how hard it was to restore his own block to that original condition once it had been grazed by sheep. So when kangaroo numbers exploded in the last few decades, putting grazing pressure on the 9ha of bushland in his care, Don invented his own kangaroo-proof fence which is not only effective but protects 'roos from harm should they try to crash through the fence. The secret is two loosely strung wires: the second and third wires from the top. The third wire is also only fixed at every second post, allowing any 'roos that do crash a fence to disentangle themselves and live to hop another day.

Silver Banksia
Banksia marginata

The Good Samaritan of Australian plants

Historically, banksias occur as sacred groves of ancient trees hidden deep in the Barossa Ranges, or on creek banks. On the valley floor their presence indicates sandy soil. These days they are doing it tough, and their natural propensity to provide nectar for wildlife is being compromised by the stresses of a warming climate.

Flora for fauna

Banksias are the 'corner store' for honeyeaters, bees, possums and insects. Their golden candle flowers provide precious food, in the form of nectar, in late summer and autumn when there is little else available; this is the ecosystem niche that plants like banksias and mistletoe fill. They are a nesting tree for Bronzewing Pigeons; also loved by White-browed Babblers.

Vital statistics

- long-lived; large trees can be hundreds of years old
- typically grow in lighter, well-drained, often sandy soils
- banksias are a fire-retardant species

Families of White-browed Babblers move seamlessly and gregariously through the canopies of banksias and Native Pine.

Best on show

- Kaiser Stuhl Conservation Park walk
- Barossa Bushgardens
- Barossa Valley Golf Club
- Sandy Creek Conservation Park walk

11

These woody seed cones are the inspiration for Snugglepot & Cuddlepie, much-loved Australian children's book characters, as well as 'loose parts' for children, and are innately interesting to touch and engage with.

Eastern Spinebill gleaning nectar from a banksia flower. The Barossa boasts some fourteen species of honeyeater. Honeyeaters may spend up to 18 hours a day feeding to satisfy their energy requirements.

Being a marsupial, Common Ringtail Possums give birth to live young and carry them around in a pouch. Generally two young are born and they remain in the mother's pouch for four months, and their eyes do not open for at least 90 days. Both parents carry them around on their backs until they are weaned at six months, by which time they are fully furred. Ringtail Possums are more common in southern Barossa. They are active at night, tending to be more common in shrubby understorey, rather than tall trees, and are specialised leaf eaters. They also eat nectar, flower buds and fruits, and will make flimsy spherical nests (called 'dreys') in the tree canopy. Ringtail Possums are smaller than the more common Brushtail Possum.

Ridge - fruited Mallee
Eucalyptus incrassata

Mallee with a future

The first eucalypt with a degree in sustainable housing, as it won't block the sun's rays shining on your solar panels: it only grows to roof height. The small gum for your home garden.

Flora for fauna
Honeyeaters and wattlebirds adore its nectar.

Design me!
- entwine Old Man's Beard (*Clematis microphylla*) up its trunk to produce showy creamy flowers in early spring

Vital statistics
- prefers sandy soils, however may grow on heavier soils

Best on show
- Barossa Bushgardens
- original trees in woodland opposite The Rex, Magnolia Rd Tanunda
- Sandy Creek Conservation Park walk

Creamy flowers in spring, with prominent, ribbed woody gumnuts in clusters of up to six.

A home among the gum trees. Ridge-fruited Mallees used as a small, sensible garden tree in Tanunda.

Let the children play! Mallees make good climbing trees with their multiple trunks, angled branches and low height.

Wattlebirds feed on eucalypt blossom as well as flowering shrubs such as this bottlebrush.

The remnant patch of locally rare Ridge-fruited Mallees in Magnolia Rd Tanunda had only two remaining seed-producing trees. Twenty years on, thanks to the efforts of people like Greg Kretschmer (shown collecting seed in photo) this woodland at Faith Lutheran College has been given new life and is thriving. Only two other significant patches of this species are thought to exist in the Barossa, at Moppa and Sandy Creek. The right plant in the right place, honouring the sense of place.

Southern Cypress-pine, Native Pine
Callitris gracilis

Barossa's sand man

Stands of Native Pine can indicate deeper sand patches at Moppa, Tanunda, Kalimna and Altona, which were once the shores of an ancient lake.[6] Also found on sandy rises in the Barossa Ranges, the wind-blown sand being a form of Loess, which makes up the topsoil for the famous Hill of Grace vineyard.

Flora for fauna

Native Pines are habitat for many woodland birds, including Bronzewing Pigeons, White-browed Babblers, Grey Shrikethrush, thornbills, wattlebirds, robins, whistlers, and parrots. Parrots seek the maturing fruit.

Vital statistics

- a tall, linear-shaped tree, long-lived, termite resistant
- in the absence of patch-burning formerly carried out by Aboriginal people and/or natural fires caused by lightning, many remaining older stands of Native Pine tend to form a closed woodland shutting out the sunlight, to the detriment of many original understorey plants

Buff-rumped Thornbill (top) and Yellow Thornbill (above). Tiny thornbills move in groups through the canopy gleaning insects off the foliage, softly calling to each other to maintain contact.

Right: Australia's Christmas tree. Native Pine woodland in sand at Barossa Valley Golf Club.

Best on show
- Barossa Bushgardens
- Altona CSR Landcare Reserve walk, Lyndoch
- Jack Bobridge Cycle Track
- heritage-listed bushland, Magnolia Rd Tanunda

15

These ripe woody Native Pine seed cones have opened to release their seed, which is eaten by galahs and cockatoos.

Red-capped Robin (top) and Hooded Robin (above). Robins need horizontal perching branches up to 1.5m off the ground from which to spot their prey on the ground. Robins are 'pouncers', meaning that they pounce on their prey from their vantage point. If there are no perches then there will be no robins. Woodland trees such as Native Pine provide this critical habitat.

Dragon Fly on Native Pine (far left). Stands of Native Pine and Blue Gum provide welcome shade on the Jack Bobridge Cycle Track: Nuriootpa-Angaston section.

Christmas Bush
Bursaria spinosa

The vineyard's friend

Plays host to beneficial insects which protect grapevines from damage; a natural control for Light Brown Apple Moth, one of the main vineyard pests. Christmas Bush takes its name from prominent sprays of sweetly perfumed, creamy flowers leading up to Christmas. A smart tactician - why would you want to flower in spring when everyone else is? Steal the show, and flower at Christmas instead!

Flora for fauna

Christmas Bush is a host plant for several beneficial wasps which attack Light Brown Apple Moth (LBAM). The tiny Dolly wasp (*Dolichogenidea tasmanica*), for instance, the most abundant parasitic wasp of LBAM, lays a single egg in the host LBAM larva (caterpillar). When the Dolly wasp egg hatches inside it starts feeding from the host body (LBAM larva) and grows, eventually killing the LBAM caterpillar. Each Dolly wasp can attack many LBAM larvae in their life span.[1]

These wasps contribute to biological pest control in vineyards throughout the year. Increasingly local native plants are being planted in and around vineyards to provide food, shelter and alternative prey to nourish natural enemies of pests, and enhance their capacity to control pests.

Design me!
- popular in vineyards both in buffers and at the end of the vine row (headland) as it attracts beneficial insects
- tip-prune each autumn to grow a denser shrub

Vital statistics
- also called 'rattle bush' locally, because of the way the two seeds rattle in their tiny purse-shaped capsule in autumn

Christmas Bush flowers in Nov/Dec. An an excellent nectar plant for all adult butterflies.

Best on show
- Barossa Bushgardens
- Gomersal Rd Rest Area

Prue Henschke, who pioneered the planting of beneficials such as Christmas Bush in vineyards.

Top left: Grapevine Moth larvae cause chewing damage to developing berries.

Top right: "Insect pests cause economic damage in Australian vineyards each season. For example, Light Brown Apple Moth (LBAM) causes damage to flower clusters, resulting in yield losses and damage to berry skins. Damaged skins provide infection sites for moulds like Botrytis cinerea, which result in a reduction in fruit quality and yield losses".[3]

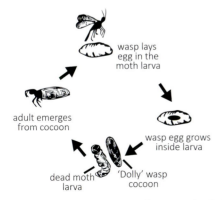

wasp lays egg in the moth larva

adult emerges from cocoon

wasp egg grows inside larva

dead moth larva

'Dolly' wasp cocoon

Life cycle of a beneficial wasp eg Dolly Wasp (Dolichogenidea tasmanica).[2]

Female Dolly Wasp (Dolichogenidea tasmanica) parasitising larval Light Brown Apple Moth (LBAM), Epiphyas postvittana.

Dryland Tea-tree
Melaleuca lanceolata

Playing possum

They are the double bass player in the woodland orchestra; unassuming but indispensable.....to possums, for instance!

Flora for fauna

Possums have a sweet tooth for the Dryland Tea-tree and will graze on its leaves and flowers quite heavily. Its summer flowers are a nectar source for butterflies and bees, and a host plant for Melaleuca Mistletoe that provides food for Satin Azure Butterfly larva.

Design me!

• the best screening plant in the Barossa

Best on show

• Moppa roadside verges
• Barossa Bushgardens

Dryland Tea-tree is easily recognised as it is one of the few natives flowering in Jan/Feb ie midsummer.

Common Brushtail Possum: how lucky are we to still have wild marsupials roaming our Barossa backyards at night, sharing our urban life-space! A thrill to be lying snug in bed and hear their throaty call just outside your bedroom window! They can be a mixed blessing, however, as they can thump around on (and in!) the roof and fancy our fruit trees. Brushtails are now more common in Barossa towns than in bushland and are a protected species. Being a marsupial, Brushtail Possums give birth to live young, usually a single jellybean-sized joey which makes its way into the mother's pouch where it will live for four to five months.

An ancient multi-stemmed Dryland Tea-tree gracing Peppermint Box woodland near Nuriootpa.

- Dryland Tea-tree/*Melaleuca lanceolata* starts as a bushy shrub and grows into a graceful small tree over decades, sometimes multi-stemmed
- its smaller cousin the Mallee Honey-myrtle/*Melaleuca brevifolia* was on the brink of local extinction, with only two remaining plants in the Barossa. It was reintroduced by sourcing seed from plants in the adjacent Marne River to the east of the Barossa, ie the nearest available seed source

Ringtail Possums are more common in Southern Barossa.

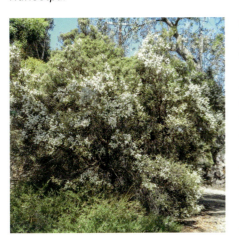

Left: playing possum! Both Ringtail Possums and to a lesser extent the larger Brushtails go crazy over Dryland Tea-tree foliage/flowers and tip-prune it quite severely. Note the damage done to the top of this normally rounded bush. Brushtail Possums' main diet is eucalypts (gum) leaves and flowers, fruit and shoots, however they will snack on birds' eggs and insects.

Right: Satin Azure Butterfly caterpillars eat the flowers and leaves of mistletoes attached to Dryland Tea-tree.

Yaccas, Grass-trees
Xanthorrhoea species

Bush ballerina

Her unique leafy skirt and elegant flower stem catch the eye. Maturity brings character and poise.

Flora for fauna

VIP habitat and protection for wildlife. Birds, butterflies, moths and insects love her vertical flower spike. Buff-rumped Thornbills are known to nest in the crown of leaves of *semiplana*.

Design me!

• Yaccas are on the 'A' list of Barossa plants and can take centre stage in any landscaping, however the first flower spike may take five years or more to develop

Vital statistics

• Yaccas live for hundreds of years
• two locally occurring species: *X. semiplana* has a broader leaf; the more diminuitive *X. quadrangulata* tends to be restricted to Barossa Ranges

Xanthorrhoea quadrangulata on a Barossa Ranges ridgeline.

Best on show

• roadside verges in the Ranges
• Hale and Kaiser Stuhl Conservation Park walks
• Barossa Bushgardens

21

Crescent Honeyeater feeding on yacca spike.

Above: Xanthorrhoea semiplana: flower spikes can grow 3-4 metres in length in a good year.
Below: Buff-rumped Thornbills nest in yacca foliage.

Grapevine Moths attending flower stem in spring.

Hakeas
Hakea species

Free spirits
Hakeas do their own thing and refuse to conform to tidy stereotypes.

Flora for fauna
Hakeas' large hard woody seed cones are probably too much trouble for even cockies to bother with. Small birds such as finches will nest in hakeas. Their main wildlife benefit seems to be as a refuge and shelter. Understorey shrubs like hakeas accumulate large amounts of leaflife beneath their canopy, so important for skinks, lizards and insects. In addition this acts as a sunscreen, thereby reducing soil moisture loss, an added bonus in the context of a warming climate.

Uses
The dark green foliage is useful to contrast with lighter shades of green in landscaping. Hard woody seed cones are useful as 'loose parts' for children.

Right: Hakea rugosa/Dwarf Hakea in flower.

Vital statistics
- Beaked Hakea/*Hakea rostrata* is a low, bushy, spreading shrub to 1m or sometimes 1.5m
- its smaller cousin the Dwarf Hakea/*Hakea rugosa* has really spiky needle-like leaves and occurs on sandy sites
- Keeled Hakea/*Hakea carinata* grows in the Barossa Ranges

Have you ever saved a plant from local extinction? Terri Bateman is credited with saving the Dwarf Hakea by collecting seed from this plant on busy Magnolia Rd Tanunda. It was one of two known remaining seed-producing plants on the Valley floor. Barossa Bushgardens then grew the plants and now they are flourishing. As a result hundreds of new plants now populate the Barossa. Terri is called the Barossa's 'Earth mother' with good reason, having devoted her life to conserving local flora.

Beaked Hakea showing woody seed cones.

Best on show

- Barossa Goldfields walks
- Barossa Bushgardens
- Hale Conservation Park walk
- roadside verges around Kaiser Stuhl Conservation Park

Right: Bearded Dragon resting in the leaflife beneath a Beaked Hakea.

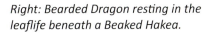

Beaked Hakea/Hakea rostrata in flower.

Red-browed Finch. Finches nest in hakeas.

Hakea's woody seed cones and seed.

Tea-trees
Leptospermum species

Generous hosts

The tea-tree family tree provides waterfront accommodation, hosting many guests: insects, bugs, beetles and spiders.

Flora for fauna

Tea-trees are a magnet for small fauna including bugs, beetles, ladybirds and spiders which prey on vineyard pests and are hence beneficial predators.

Vital statistics

- two of the three local species like to be near water
- Silky Tea-tree/*Leptospermum lanigerum* likes a permanently damp site
- Prickly Tea-tree/*Leptospermum continentale* likes a damp site
- Heath Tea-tree/*Leptospermum myrsinoides* on drier, higher sites, sandy soils

Best on show

- Kaiser Stuhl Conservation Park walk
- Barossa Bushgardens
- Tanunda Creek
- Altona CSR Landcare Reserve walk

Prickly Tea-tree is common in the Barossa Ranges on seasonally damp sites, generally near or on a creekline, and is home to many beneficial insects such as Damsel Bugs, Transverse and Eleven-spotted Ladybird Beetles, Brown Lacewing adults and Predatory Shield Bugs, which help control a range of vineyard pests.[4]

Left: the Predatory Shield Bug can often be found on some species of tea-trees, and is a key predator of a range of vineyard pests including Light Brown Apple Moth.[5]

Right: Heath Tea-tree in flower.

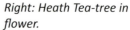

Silky Tea-tree is found right on the water's edge.

Huntsman Spiders live under loose bark or on foliage and are commonly found in Barossa homes eg walking across walls, or cruising across your car dashboard! They are easily relocated to alternative outside accommodation by placing an upturned glass over them and sliding a piece of paper across the top of the glass, thereby trapping them inside. They are beneficial insofar as they feed on insects such as cockroaches and crickets and are not generally aggressive or harmful to humans, but they can bite. Prickly Tea-tree plays host to a broad range of spiders: Huntsman, Wolf, Orb-weaving, Long-jawed, Flower, Ground and Jumping Spiders.[6]

Transverse Ladybird Beetle is another good bug in vineyards, found on some species of tea-trees.

Left: this cute Jumping Spider is a cunning and agile predator in the vineyard, and uses tea-trees as B&B accommodation; they are 5-15mm long and move quickly! They are active hunters and will feed on key vineyard pests, and are hence considered beneficial.

Golden Wattle
Acacia pycnantha

The sprinter

Boasts that it can outgrow any plant in the Barossa. And did you know that Golden Wattle is Australia's floral emblem, and the reason we wear green and gold at the Olympics?

Flora for fauna

Bronzewing pigeons and other birds seek out wattle seed and can be found foraging for it in the leaflife beneath the wattle. Nesting tree for bronzewings, who also act as seed-dispersers. Nectar source for honeyeaters, insects, bees. Bearded Dragons perch motionless on branches pretending not to be seen. Golden Wattles are territory markers for the dominant male kangaroos who rub the scent glands on their chest up and down the young wattle, damaging it in the process.[7]

Design me!

Useful in landscaping for instant effect as it has a phenomenally fast growth rate and may be two metres tall in a couple of years.

Vital statistics

- grows to 6-8 metres in both clay and sandy soils
- lives 10-15 years or longer; colonizes bare ground eg after fire
- resin exuding from the trunk and branches can be eaten as a take-away snack but beware: it may glue your teeth together!

Golden Wattles are homes, beds and supermarkets for Bronzewing Pigeons.

"This is the Golden Wattle,
'Tis the emblem of our land,
You can put it in a bottle
Or hold it in your hand."

(C19 verse, author unknown).

Wattles are one of the first plants to blossom in spring.

Self-sown Golden Wattle on the edge of a vineyard.

White-throated Treecreeper spiralling up the trunk of a Golden Wattle gleaning insects from the bark.

Wattle Blue Butterfly breeds on wattles, ie it is a host plant for caterpillars of this butterfly.

Let the children play

Celebrate Wattle Day Sept 1st by counting the different wattles in bloom and collecting sprigs of wattle flowers.

Best on show

- Barossa Bushgardens

Kangaroo Thorn
Acacia paradoxa

A prickly customer

This bird magnet is a 'tough love' mother. Beneath her harsh exterior lies a heart of gold, as she selflessly protects the small woodland birds beneath her skirts.

Flora for fauna

Habitat heaven for blue wrens and small woodland birds which love the safety of her dense prickly foliage to nest and feed in. Shady refuge and master bedroom for kangaroos to sleep under during the day by scraping out a shallow dustbowl to lay in. Foraging kangaroos nibble the tips in summer when there is precious little other food.

Design me!
- plant this shrub if you want to attract small native birds such as wrens and honeyeaters
- good screening shrub

Best on show
- Barossa Ranges roadsides eg Tanunda - Angaston scenic route / Menglers Hill lookout
- Barossa Bushgardens

Right: Kangaroo Thorn typically grows to 2 metres, occasionally taller.

Blue wrens need dense shrubs for their survival.

Nature's windfall: by trapping falling gum leaves as well as contributing its own leaflife, understorey shrubs such as Kangaroo Thorn contribute to the greater good. Leaflife is Nature's sunscreen, minimising soil moisture loss, thereby sustaining our plants, as well as turning into healthy new soil

Blossom provides a nectar source for birds in spring.

Eastern Spinebill feeding on Eremophila flower. Some fourteen species of honeyeater exist in the Barossa and wattles and Eremophilas are important habitat and food sources.

"Delicate mother kangaroo....
Lifting her beautiful slender face...
Her sensitive, long, pure-bred face.
Her full antipodal eyes, so dark,
So big and quiet and remote, having watched so many empty dawns in silent Australia."

D H Lawrence, "Kangaroo"

Swamp Wattle
Acacia retinodes

Strappy elegance
Sentinel flag of the bush, whose faintly stirring leaves signal a refreshing Acacia breeze.[8]

Flora for fauna
Provides food for the Icilius Blue Butterfly as the caterpillars eat the young leaves. Birds such as pigeons adore its seed and both rosellas and possums enjoy eating the cream flowers.

Vital statistics
- small tree to 5-7m. Two local varieties: the Valley floor variety prefers a damp site, often found near water; the Hills form may occur on drier, elevated ground in the Barossa Ranges and flowers more profusely
- distinctive dark trunk, upright form; yellow flowers Nov/Dec
- some wattles are cultivated for their seed of different flavours which is ground into wattleseed coffee and biscuits

Hills form of Swamp Wattle in flower at Boehm Springs.

Best on show
- along the riverbanks of the North and South Para Rivers
- Boehm Springs Reserve near Springton

Icilius Blue Butterfly. The caterpillars eat the young leaves.

Wattle seed.

Ruby Saltbush and friends
Enchylaena tomentosa

Nature's tablecloth

Nature's tablecloth, covering the ground in a dense mat, occurring both as groundcovers and small shrubs.

Flora for fauna
The red, orange or yellow berries are eagerly sought by lizards, skinks, honeyeaters and other birds.

Go foraging for ripe berries in late summer/autumn; they may be eaten raw and are quite palatable. Bush tucker.

Vital statistics
- Ruby Saltbush/*Enchlyaena tomentosa* comes in two forms: either as a small dense shrub to 1m, or as a prostrate groundcover
- Nodding Saltbush/*Einadia nutans* has delicate pixie-like leaves, with tiny red berries
- Fragrant Saltbush/*Rhagodia parabolica* is a rounded, robust shrub
- Berry Saltbush/*Atriplex semibaccata*; groundcover

Design me!
- saltbush are fire-resistant
- as an infill plant in landscaping, covering the ground and eliminating most weeds because of its dense habit

Best on show
- Peter Lehmann Wines riverbank garden
- Gomersal Rd Rest Area, Tanunda

Fragrant Saltbush: the male plant has grape-like clusters of small red fruit.

Ruby Saltbush is easily identified by its edible berries and succulent leaves.

White-plumed Honeyeater on a vineyard dripline. Honeyeaters will shamelessly gorge themselves on Ruby Saltbush berries, throwing their heads back and nearly choking in the process of getting them down.

Sennas or Cassias
Senna artemisioides subspecies

"Happy chappies"

Sennas brighten up the bush and tend to smile a lot, especially in Oct/Nov. which is 'party time', when they come out in swathes of yellow flowers. A wise choice for the Barossa as they occur from here northwards and will cope with a warming climate.

Flora for fauna
Birds eat the fallen seed; ants eat the arils only and help disperse the seed. Sennas are a caterpillar food plant for the Small Grass Yellow and Icilius Blue Butterflies, also a source of nectar.

Vital statistics
- there are three common subspecies of *Senna artemisioides* in the Barossa, namely *artemisioides*, *coriacea*, and *petiolaris*
- small to medium, round shrub from 1 - 2m in height
- found on poor soils such as calcareous limey sands, but also does well on clay

Right: the petiolaris form, which boasts jointed needles rather than leaves.

Far right: Small Grass Yellow Butterfly larva on Senna leaf.

Small Grass Yellow Butterfly: its caterpillars feed on young Senna leaves.

Senna artemisioides ssp. *petiolaris* at Barossa Bushgardens.

Best on show
- Barossa Bushgardens
- Gomersal Rd Rest Area, Tanunda

Bottlebrushes
Callistemon species

The giddy aunt

Bottlebrushes are very much their own person, with a slightly crazy streak and their infectious love of life.

Flora for fauna

Honeyeater heaven. Wattlebirds, lorikeets and honeyeaters feast on nectar in the flowers. Koalas also browse on bottlebrushes.

Vital statistics

- generally prefers a damp site or at least one which is seasonally damp, except *C. teretifolius* which occurs on drier hilly sites in Southern Barossa;
Scarlet Bottlebrush/
C. rugulosus;
River Bottlebrush/*C. sieberi*;
Flinders Ranges Bottlebrush/
C. teretifolius

Best on show

- River Bottlebrush – magnificent specimens on banks of Bethany Creek at Bethany Reserve
- Barossa Bushgardens
- Hale Conservation Park walk

Scarlet Bottlebrush.

Rainbow Lorikeet raid.

Flinders Ranges Bottlebrush.

River Bottlebrush has cream flowers.

Wildlife in Vineyards

How refreshing to know that vineyards are also home to an array of wildlife which is adopting and adapting to such a modified environment. Two things are happening here:

- wildlife is moving in naturally, exploiting opportunities: for example kangaroos, choughs and Bearded Dragons; plus mid-row plantings of native grasses are a food source for Red-rumped Parrots, Bronzewing and Crested Pigeons, thornbills and finches
- vignerons are working with Nature, and actively encouraging beneficial insects by introducing local native plants (such as Christmas Bush, Tea-trees, native grasses) into vineyards. These beneficial bugs and insects are predators of vineyard pests.

Tawny Frogmouths day-roosting in the vineyard. Being nocturnal hunters, frogmouths and owls rest during the day and pretend not to be seen by staying breathtakingly still.

Bearded Dragons climb up into the canopy to sun themselves on the vineyard posts which no doubt serve as de facto trees! They lay there quite motionless and even track around the post to follow the sun. They happily eat white-snails.

Do sheep get tipsy? Sheep are turned into the vineyard to keep the grass down after harvest in April, usually for 3-4 weeks of crash-grazing, but sometimes they are left there from April until just before bud-burst in August. Sheep take care of serious weeds such as fat hen, marshmallow and mustard weed.[1] High stocking rates are preferred lest the cunning sheep cherry-pick the grasses and leave the weeds! Their hoof compaction pushes the seed of native grasses such as wallaby grass onto the soil, creating the necessary 'seed soil contact' required for germination. Sheep grazing also reduces more costly inputs such as slashing with tractors and herbicide usage.

Free-range geese in the vineyard. Geese do a lot of cleaning up of weeds such as milk thistle, barley grass and rye grass.

Chough in vineyard defending its chick (foreground) with a threat display.

Winery-hopping. Gregarious family groups of White-winged Choughs move seamlessly back and forth between patches of woodland and adjacent vineyards where they account for countless earwigs and other bugs, to the delight of savvy viticulturists. Choughs scratch and peck away like chooks at the straw mulch beneath the vines with their beaks and claws. The straw also attracts mice, which in turn are preyed upon by brown snakes, and many a vineyard worker has eyeballed a brown snake at close quarters when checking the driplines beneath the vines.

Necessity is the mother of invention. Bronzewing Pigeon nesting in vines.

Kangaroos will scratch out a daytime resting pad in the straw beneath the vines. Smart roos even select an east-west running row, laying down on the southern side so they are in shade all day long without having to move.

Local Western Grey Kangaroo with joey in pouch. Roos eat the grass under the drippers but can also cause damage by taking young leaves and shoots and by eating the grapes.

Hares and rabbits can decimate young vines.

Red-rumped Parrots forage for grass seeds in the vine mid-rows.

Wild in the Barossa

......*it takes an entire landscape to sustain our wildlife.*

The symbol of endurance, foraging echidnas still call the Barossa home. Note the disturbed ground from its diggings in search of grubs, beetles, earthworms, insect larvae, ants and termites. Echidnas go solo most of the year except for mating season, and have a large home range of up to 192ha. Core habitat in the Barossa centres around areas of undisturbed bushland in conservation parks. Echidnas are egg-laying mammals, in the same family as the platypus (monotremes) and produce only one young every 3 to 5 years, called a puggle (see page 43).[2]

The much-loved and commonly seen Laughing Kookaburra.

A flashmob of Galahs. Galahs are the Spitfire pilots of the bush and can get up to some crazy aerobic acrobatics. They have adapted to agricultural landscapes, and have expanded their range, 'following the plough' as a result of European settlement.

Baby kooka's daily diet
- as observed [3]

- ***thirty skinks, (substituted with worms, after rain)***
- ***numerous grubs and beetles***
- ***occasional treats: a yabbie; small and baby birds eg wrens and pigeons; a half-grown rat***

Peregrine Falcon in flight. The Peregrine Falcon has been shown to be a good ecological barometer of the health of the environment as they are exclusively bird-eaters and at the top of the food chain. Refer breeding territories on inside front cover map. Territories are large areas that the birds defend against intruders because these are their breeding and foraging areas that they depend on. The improvement in falcon populations is put down to the decline in organochlorine chemical (DDT, DDD and dieldrin) contamination.

On a wing and a prayer:
Peregrine Falcon numbers increasing locally

A good news story: based on official data, there are now twelve breeding pairs in the Barossa, compared with only six in the early 1980s.[4] During the 1950s and 1960s, Peregrine Falcon populations experienced a dramatic decline in many countries in the world including parts of Australia due to reproductive failures involving thin-shelled and broken eggs caused by DDT chemicals in the environment after these pesticides were ingested by the falcons in their prey.[5] Being at the top of the food chain Peregrine Falcons are particularly susceptible to accumulating large quantities of pesticides. Since many of these pesticides have been banned and are no longer used, the Peregrine Falcon population has recovered and is one of the great wildlife success stories.[6]

The Yellow-tailed Black Cockatoo is the largest Australian cockatoo, a welcome sight flying overhead. Flocks are extending their range northwards into the Barossa Ranges from the Adelaide Hills, feeding on the seeds of banksias, yaccas, sheoaks and hakeas. Their powerful bills bite into the seed cones. Their growing presence in the Barossa may be due to the pine plantations of the Southern Barossa, as they have adapted to feed on introduced pines.

The rare Rosenberg's or Heath Goanna in a garden near Williamstown.

Chris Steeles and Megan Coles like saving birds so they formed a Landcare group and began building and erecting bird nest boxes. Fifteen in the first year, and they soon had Adelaide Rosella chicks; they now have twenty-five boxes up and about forty chicks in a season, with a 95% occupancy rate, mainly Adelaide Rosellas, Ringtail Possums and bats. Their influence has extended across the region, inspiring others to follow suit.

"Mummy, mummy, dinosaur!" came the cry from the verandah as Jacky checked on her two year old. "Too much screen time," she mused as she brought him inside. But next day the very same excited cry had her running onto the verandah to find her baby pointing at a rather large goanna lumbering through the garden, several metres away. Barossa backyards down Sandy Creek way can have interesting playmates. Nearby Sandy Creek, Hale and Warren Conservation Parks are core habitat for goannas. The photo shows a Sand Goanna at Altona.

Eastern Rosella raising chicks in a nestbox.

Wildlife in Rivers and Creeks

The North and South Para Rivers and their tributaries feeding in from the high country of the Barossa Ranges are the lifelines of the Barossa, both connecting and nurturing the landscape as wildlife corridors. The westward-flowing rivers join and flow into Gulf St Vincent via the Port Gawler mangroves.

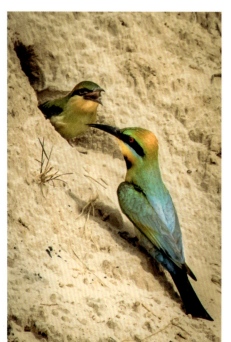

The Clamorous Reed Warbler is a migratory bird that flies in every September from northern Australia and beyond, spending summer breeding in the riverbeds of the Para River and its tributaries, before heading north again in March. Reeds and Bulrushes provide core habitat as nesting sites, as well as shelter and food. This cheeky but shy bird has a distinctive high-pitched melodious call; "twitchy-twitchy-twitchy quarty-quarty-quarty" [8] and is usually heard before it is seen. Go down to the riverbank anywhere along the North or South Para Rivers over summer to hear their melodious calls and see them playing hide-and-seek with you.

The tale of three migratory birds which all rely on the river

Rainbow Bee-eaters (left) arrive each September to breed in holes in steep sandy sections of riverbank, then wing it all the way back to northern Australia each March. They excavate their own burrows into the banks of creeks and mounds with their beaks, up to a metre long with a larger chamber at the end of the tunnel. The female seems to do most of the work, excavating a burrow in a few days. The tunnel opening is a tight fit for the birds and appears to be tailor-made to suit.[7] They can be seen flitting from tall gums out into the air to snatch a flying insect and then returning to their perch.

Sacred Kingfishers migrate here every September from northern Australia.

Tim Scheiner has overseen the renaissance of riverbank plantings along Jacob's Creek, putting the local plants back where they belong. This creates habitat and contributes to greater connectivity along Barossa rivers.

Some 290 permanent pools such as this one in Tanunda provide habitat through summer for wildlife including birds, as well as native fish, freshwater shrimp, yabbies and Long-necked Turtles. The South Para River still has populations of sea-going native fish such as Climbing Galaxias and Congolli.

Downstream on the North Para - Kingsford pools.

Dry creekbed, Tanunda Creek.

Wild Leaflife

Leaflife is the unsung hero of the bush. It has a life of its own and supports so much other life. It used to be called 'leaf litter' and consists of fallen bark, twigs, seeds and dead leaves.

- Nature's sunscreen, protecting bare ground and thereby reducing soil moisture loss, conserving precious moisture for plants
- Habitat for all sorts of bugs, skinks, beetles, worms, spiders, moths and detritus feeders
- Leaflife is 'soil in the act of becoming!' It improves soil quality as organic matter breaks down into new soil.

Foraging echidna. Bushland produces large quantities of wild leaflife, ideal for echidnas, where there are dense understorey shrubs for protection and where they can forage in the ground, in dead wood, under loose bark and leaves.[10] If disturbed they readily bunker down against a tree trunk or dig into the leaflife, instantly camouflaged.

An echidna puggle photographed within the nursery burrow, using a special camera. The mother returns to the burrow every five days to feed and clean the puggle. Dead leaves and other detritus form a natural protective layer around the growing echidna which lives in a torpor with lowered metabolism between feeds, until weaning at seven months, when the mother opens the burrow and brings her young outside. From that moment on the young echidna is totally on its own.[9]

Giant earthworms in Barossa woodlands can grow up to half a metre in length. They are only found in undisturbed bushland under trees.

Young Rosenberg's Goanna scuttling across the floor of silent leaves.[12]

Sundew/Drosera herbfield in undisturbed woodland, Marananga.

Bibron's Toadlet's habitat is open grasslands and wooded areas; eggs are usually laid in shallow depressions and dry creekbeds and covered with damp leaves.

Wildlife in Dams

Wildlife has adapted to our dams, with some 1 790 spread across the North Para catchment alone, providing water for life.[11] There are large dams, small dams, farm dams, winery dams, as well as reservoirs. By late summer both the dams and the few remaining permanent pools in the watercourses become critical refugia for local wildlife. From kangaroos to yabbies, Nankeen Night Herons to Galahs, Hooded Robins at Moppa and wild Emus at Eden Valley, they all need water to survive.

Farm dam in Barossa Ranges with Pale Rush/Juncus pallidus, one of our largest rushes.

Top right: immature Nankeen Night Heron. They rest in thick shrubbery and sheoaks on the edges of Barossa dams.

Bottom right: pair of Wood Ducks on dam; Wood Ducks graze on native grasses and nest in tree hollows.

Yabbies hibernate in tunnels below the water table for months at a time to survive when dams and semi-permanent pools dry up. They excavate a tunnel, go in and then plug it up.

Common Froglet, found in and around dams, or in damp areas near streams.

Red-bellied Black Snake 'periscoping' us from the safety of the dam. They spend a lot of time in the water, and feed on frogs and small mammals. They are considered a shy snake, although venomous.

Dam in summer.

Native Currant
Acrotriche depressa

Lost property

An inconspicuous chap, not on anyone's menu much and hard to find these days.

Flora for fauna

A mystery shrub, as the plentiful fruit is not always eaten and remains on the plant, although kangaroos graze its prickly leaves. What might have once dined here? Locally extinct mammals such as potoroos, Brush-tailed Bettongs and the Tammar Wallaby? Or the now rare Southern Brown Bandicoot? Also ground-dwelling birds such as quail and Emus, both now scarce in the Barossa. Possums, lizards, currawongs and ravens would be other contenders today, as well as introduced foxes.

Vital statistics

- burgundy-coloured fruit clusters the size of a small bunch of grapes are arranged around the branch on pendulous stalks

Clusters of fruit, which has a strong tangy flavour and makes excellent jelly and jam.

Native Currant bush. "Once German settlers learned about them, they developed a tradition of annual picnics when families would spend a day in the bush, gathering the berries to make preserves and cordials. This widespread custom dates back to at least 1856. Some of the berry-pickers grew impatient with the painful process of extracting the berries from the prickly lower branches and pulled up the bushes roots and all, in order to harvest the crop more easily!"[1]

47

Food for thought: who would have dined on Native Currant in days gone by.....? Four likely suspects:

Long-nosed Potoroo (above). Native Currant would have been 'low-hanging fruit' for potoroos, now locally extinct. Their diet consists of fungi, also tubers, soil arthropods (insects and spiders), seeds, fruit and vegetation.[2]

Possums (top right) were once more common and widespread than today and are fruit eaters, so they could have accounted for more of the crop in days gone by. Brushtail Possums will graze at ground level.

Emu (centre). Native Currant seeds have been found in Emu scats: there are wild Emus in nearby Para Wirra Conservation Park, and a pair of wild Emus recently raised seven chicks near Eden Valley.

The Tammar Wallaby (bottom right) is now locally extinct but still thrives on Kangaroo Island.

Best on show
- Barossa Goldfields walks
- Hale Conservation Park walk
- Sandy Creek Conservation Park walk

Mistletoe
Amyema & Lysiana species

Hitchhiker

The hanger-on, enjoys a free ride, but hey he's part of the bigger picture and is a true-blue local. Well tolerated in small doses but tries to take over the party by monopolising entire trees and has to be cut down to size.

Flora for fauna

Mistletoe is spread by the Mistletoebird (and others) which eats the fruit, digests it and then straddles a branch and poops out the seed onto it.[3] The sticky seed then attaches itself to a branch of a tree or shrub. Mistletoe is an example of a parasite which relies upon a host (often a gum tree) and a bird to disperse the seed. The plant is an important food source in late summer when there is little other nectar around for many birds; Diamond Firetails and Musk Lorikeets are just two local species which raid Mistletoe. Also a nesting site owing to its dense foliage.

Vital statistics

- two local varieties: Box Mistletoe/*Amyema miquelii* only grows on eucalypts;

Harlequin Mistletoe/*Lysiana exocarpi* does not grow on eucalypts but prefers sheoaks

Best on show

- widespread on Barossa roadside gums, often in excessive numbers owing to the lack of other trees and shrubs to act as hosts and share the load

Satin Azure Butterfly is one of several species of butterfly whose caterpillars eat the flowers and leaves of mistletoes.

Box Mistletoe often droops pendulously from the branch of its host. Possums not only like grazing mistletoe leaves and flowers, but will break off pieces of the plant whilst feeding, having a similar effect to pruning. Ringtail Possums also build their dens (flimsy nests) in its protective foliage.

Above: male Mistletoebird. The Mistletoebird/Mistletoe relationship is a fine example of how the plant needs the bird, and the bird needs the plant: the bird feeds on the fruit, and in return the plant receives free seed transportation services! A symbiotic relationship.

Below: this used to be an apple! Musk Lorikeets are tenacious raiders of fruit in orchards and mistletoe is also high on their list.

Mistle-two-in-one! In a freak of Nature this Harlequin Mistletoe (top of photo with single red flowers) has piggybacked on and attached itself to the Box Mistletoe (bottom of photo) which in turn has attached itself to a host gum tree. Harlequin Mistletoe cannot attach itself directly onto eucalypts, only to species such as sheoaks and Native Cherry.

Mistletoe fruit containing the seed which is eaten by the bird, thereby spreading the plant far and wide.

Running Postman
Kennedia prostrata

Barossa cuisine

This gourmet treat for hungry beasts comes from the tastiest plant of the pea family, whose red flowers are irresistible.

Flora for fauna
With an all-consuming passion, Shingleback Lizards feast on the bright red flowers.

Vital statistics
- groundcover, prefers sunny open position on a raised bank
- lipstick-red flowers in spring

Best on show
- Barossa Bushgardens

Above: gourmet treat for hungry beasts! Shingleback Lizard at lunch.

Left: red letter day for lizards!

"What other selfless host
Puts on a foodie feast
With all you can eat!
Only to be consumed
As part of the treat?"

Old Man's Beard
Clematis microphylla

Spring showpony

This native climber is a rank opportunist. Uses other plants as a stepladder to stardom to steal the spring spotlight.

Flora for fauna
Seed clusters with their fluffy white wings provide nesting material for birds, and the plant's bushy foliage provides sheltered habitat.

Vital statistics
- naturally uses other shrubs as a step-ladder; long-lived
- leaves were warmed or bruised and then applied as a poultice for rheumatism and skin sores by Aboriginal people

Best on show
- Barossa Bushgardens
- Jack Bobridge Cycle Track, adjacent St Hallett Wines
- Angaston Primary School fence

Design me!
- plant at the base of shrubs or mallees and watch me clamber up them to grab the spotlight

Bush weaving with Old Man's Beard and Kangaroo Grass, created by students at Nuriootpa Community Children's Centre.

One of the first plants to flower and herald spring, providing a delicate display until wind and the autumn rains disperse the fluffy seeds.

Below: Old Man's Beard loves a fence.

Iron Grass
Lomandras

A rough diamond
A country lad, a larrikin, but with aspirations of being a famous artist one day. A late developer. Gregarious, likes to be in the crowd.

Flora for fauna
Lomandra seed is eaten by lizards; food source for the Phigalia Skipper Butterfly larvae.

Design me!
- in demand as a landscaping plant: plant in clumps, or in long rows at 1.2-1.4m spacings for stunning effect

Iron grass/Lomandra multiflora ssp. dura occurs in symmetrical circular clumps with pendulous strappy leaf stalks. The small seed stalks are clearly visible in the centre of the plant.

Vital statistics
- a key component of the open grassy woodlands which once graced the Barossa
- Mat-rush or Iron grass/ *Lomandra multiflora* ssp. *dura*, *Lomandra densiflora* and other local species belong to the lily family and are not technically a grass at all
- grows in both sand and clay soils
- thrives in full sun; long-lived

Best on show
- roadside verges, particularly in Moppa region
- Barossa Bushgardens

Shingleback Lizards eat the seed.

Lomandras planted on weedmat to enhance seed collection at Barossa Bushgardens.

Food plant for the Phigalia Skipper Butterfly: the caterpillars eat the leaves.

Muntries
Kunzea pomifera

Beachcombers

For Muntries, life's a beach! Muntries are a coastal plant in Australia, commonly found on dunes. The Barossa Valley floor was once an ancient lake and shoreline dunes still exist in the sandy soils around Tanunda, Moppa, Kalimna and Altona. This is where Muntries thrive, still yearning for the beach.

Flora for fauna
Lizards and birds eat fruit; a valuable food source for native bees; nectar source for butterflies.

Vital statistics
- go foraging! Muntries fruit (munterberries) are tasty and have an apple flavour. German settlers made apple-flavoured puddings from the fruit, which ripens in January
- groundcover with long runners that will take root
- showy cream flowers late spring

Design me!
- Muntries can be trellised successfully

Muntries in flower.

Best on show
- Barossa Bushgardens 'Truly Australian Front Garden'
- Altona CSR Landcare Reserve walk
- Sandy Creek Conservation Park walk

Muntries growing wild between the fairways at Barossa Valley Golf Club. Muntries send out long runners that take root.

Cotton Groundsel
Senecio pinnatifolius

A little ray of sunshine
Draws a crowd and creates a buzz of helpful activity.

Flora for fauna

Cotton Groundsel is a host plant for a variety of insects such as European honey bees, native bees and hoverflies, which are good to have around our vegie gardens. They may well all utilize the floral resources provided by groundsels, and their populations thereby benefit locally from its presence in the landscape. Hoverfly adults feed on pollen and nectar of various flowering plants but their larvae are predatory, primarily preying on aphids. Many species of aphids are common pests of a range of vegetables and other garden plants, and hence their management in gardens benefits from hoverfly presence.[4]

Design me!

• useful to plant around your vegie patch/wicking beds. Suggest a mass-planting to maximise the chance of this delightful herb self-sowing adjacent your vegie garden to provide ongoing pest control

Best on show

• Barossa Bushgardens

Groundsels are probably pollinated by a number of insects, including hoverflies, native bees, and the feral European honey bee. They are nectar plants for butterflies and native wasps.

Native bee hotel: five star accommodation for our tiny helpful insect friends. Bear in mind that half the bee species, including the most useful ones in the vegie patch, nest in the ground. So leave some bare soil and don't mulch everything.

Native Blue-banded Bees (refer photo) are perhaps the most commonly known native bee. It is the tiny Furrow Bee (Halictidae), however, which is attracted to groundsels. They are ground-nesting bees and the most abundant native bee in vegetable crops. Planting groundsels alongside your vegies may attract these bees. As native bees can only fly shorter distances from their nest than European bees, you may be able to 'tether' them to a vegie garden by your choice of companion plants. To attract native bees, plant yellow, white or blue-flowered plants.[6]

Mass-planting of Cotton Groundsel at Barossa Bushgardens. Cotton Groundsel flowers in July, with masses of bright yellow flowers. Cotton Groundsel could make a bright addition to any garden insectarium. An insectarium is simply a range of different species planted adjacent your vegie garden to optimise the chances of ongoing pest control by creating a 'reservoir' of beneficial insects, all of which have pests of their own but which don't attack the vegie garden plants. An insectarium allows beneficial insects to build up their numbers, as flowers are attractive to a range of insects because of their colour, scents and most importantly, their rewards: pollen and nectar.[5]

Right: Hoverfly on Christmas Bush/ Bursaria spinosa flower.

Wallaby Grass
Rytidosperma species

The woodland's carpet

An accommodating welcome mat with her feathery seed heads and gentle tussocks.

Flora for fauna

Wallaby grass was one of the key components of the vast herbfields which once graced the Barossa's open grassy woodlands, and is important for a wide range of wildlife: birds, butterflies, insects, kangaroos. Seedheads are a food source for seed-eating birds such as finches and pigeons. Athletic finches will first polevault grass stalks to the ground to access and eat the tasty seedhead! Wood Duck graze on native grasses.

Design me!

- can be cultivated as a native lawn provided mowing height is kept to 50mm or higher
- wallaby grasses are a basic ingredient in any 'pebbly garden' as they love to colonise beneath small pebbles and will self-sow readily once established. Hand sow in April/May

Wallaby grass being harvested in mid-row vine plantings. Native grass is extremely drought tolerant and has a variety of mechanisms for drought avoidance, either entering a prolonged dormancy or having a below-ground crown which is capable of surviving dry conditions and grazing. Native grasses are usually advantaged by the impact of drought, low rainfall and dry conditions, and become more prevalent following dry conditions.[7]

Vital statistics

- local species include *Rytidosperma setacea, caespitosa, geniculata, linkii* (much larger form)
- prefers semi-shade as it traditionally grows in open woodland

Wallaby grass in seed: distinguishable from other tussocky native grasses by its distinctive tiny twinned seedhead which resembles a wallaby's ears when plucked.

Best on show

- Barossa Bushgardens
- Barossa Valley Golf Course
- roadside verges

57

Viticulturist Dan Falkenberg among mid-row plantings of wallaby grass in an Eden Valley vineyard. Long-lived, deep-rooted perennials such as wallaby grass are used in the mid-row between the vines as they draw less moisture than other plants and improve soil texture and water absorption. The grass's root system provides pathways for moisture penetration and harbours vital soil biota for a healthy living soil, reducing the need for any form of soil cultivation and reducing compacted soil. There are also reduced maintenance costs, eg less slashing, less herbicide use for pest control, and no need to rotary hoe.

Beneficial insects such as this Brown Lacewing/Micromus tasmaniae are a beneficial arthropod in vineyards. Brown Lacewing adults are particularly abundant in wallaby grass, one of its host plants.[8] The larva of Brown Lacewing is a predator of a wide range of pests including aphids, moth eggs and small larvae, scales and whiteflies. That's why they are beneficial insects. The adults are not pests, they don't feed on plants. If they are abundant in some places it's a good sign.[9]

Red-browed Finches bobbing around happily on wallaby grass grazed short by kangaroos.

Wallaby grass is a caterpillar food plant for two butterfly species and favoured plant for this Marbled Xenica Butterfly.

Kangaroo Grass
Themeda triandra

Jekyll and Hyde

A real tussocky stunner in summer with her long showy seed stalks but needs a good haircut in autumn to avoid looking like she's had a night on the tiles. Invisible over winter months as this perennial grass reduces to a tussock until spring. There is a less common "blue 'roo" variety that has much lighter blue-coloured foliage.

Flora for fauna
Food plant for Southern Grass Dart Butterfly; grasses are great habitat for quail.

Vital statistics
- sun-loving summer-growing grass which produces tall seed stalks to 1 metre
- the long black seed tail (or awn) will turn like the hands of a clock if the seed head is implanted into potting soil and then watered. This is Nature's way of drilling the seed into the ground

Best on show
- Barossa Bushgardens
- occasionally on Barossa roadsides in summer months

Southern Grass Dart Butterfly breeds on Kangaroo Grass. The caterpillars eat the leaves.

Kangaroo Grass, showing the rarer 'blue roo' variety in the foreground, with the more common rust-coloured variety surrounding it.

Photo of plaque at Light Pass commemorating Capt. Charles Sturt's 1844 expedition passing through the Barossa.

"...the grass waving in luxuriant abundance."

Sturt's journal contains numerous references to the abundance of native grass.[10]

"Whose boast is not: 'we live' but 'we survive'"
AD Hope 'Australia'

Kangaroo Grass is a hardy, tussocky grass that still survives and thrives on Barossa roadsides. Its rusty colour in summer catches the eye.

Seed heads appear over summer and ripen by January.

Stubble Quail are known to 'explode out of the grass' when disturbed by passing humans.

Lemon-scented Grass *Cymbopogon ambiguus*
Spear Grass *Austrostipa species*

A wild child or two from the grassy woodlands

Flora for fauna

Native grasses are grazed by kangaroos, seed is eaten by birds such as finches, and they are caterpillar food plants for various butterflies. Native grasslands provide critical habitat for finches and ground-dwelling birds such as quail.

Best on Show

• Barossa Bushgardens

Lemon-scented Grass/Cymbopogon ambiguus. *Native grasses will self-colonise and thrive in pebbly gardens such as this. Grass seeds just love the microclimate created by the small river pebbles which provide moisture niches and lessen weed competition.*

Tall Spear Grass/ Austrostipa nodosa closeup.

The male Diamond Firetail finch performs a "grass stem ballet" in which he holds a long piece of dry grass in his beak, flies to his chosen lady friend, puffs out his chest, extends his neck and performs a vigorous ritual of bobbing up and down repeatedly waving the long grass stalk back and forth in his beak. When given the nod of approval he flies off to add the grass to the nest! [11]

Reeds and Sedges

A calming presence

Reeds and sedges are the river's confidante and wiser soulmate, tempering the river's excesses and exerting a stabilising and soothing influence.

Flora for fauna

Reeds are habitat heaven. Frogs such as the Spotted Marsh Frog use reeds and sedges for shelter. *Cyperus* sedges and other plants whose long stalks overhang the water provide useful attachment points for frogs' eggs – especially Ewing's Tree Frog and the Common Froglet. Reeds and sedges growing out of the water are also useful for some frogs (Eastern Banjo Frog and Spotted Marsh Frog) to attach their foam nests to. The migratory Clamorous Reed Warbler nests in riverbed reeds.

Design me!

- reeds and sedges are great landscaping plants, used as edge plants setting off a lawn, a 'frog bog' or an entry path. Can be trimmed hard and will re-shoot vigorously

Vital statistics

- Knobby Club Rush/*Ficinia nodosa*: large clumped rush with distinctive brown knobby seedheads; widely used in landscaping
- sedges/*Cyperus vaginatus, gymnocaulos*
- rushes/*Juncus subsecundus, kraussii* and *pallidus,* the largest rush
- naturally occur on damp sites and creekbanks

Foam nest of Spotted Marsh Frog eggs, guarded by sentries of sedges. Females typically lay around 1400 eggs and young frogs take 3-5 months to develop.

Left: Spotted Marsh Frog is commonly found living in and around farm dams. They typically seek refuge in grasses, reeds and sedges during the day.

Best on show

- Barossa Bushgardens
- creeklines

Finger Rush/Juncus subsecundus. Reeds and sedges, groundcovers and small bushes that grow in and around wet/ moist areas also provide frog habitat.

"Still glides the stream, and shall forever glide." (Wordsworth). An idyllic stretch of Tanunda Creek lined with sedges (Cyperus species) and Silky Tea-tree's soft grey foliage in the background.

Knobby Club Rush/Ficinia nodosa.

Spiny Flat-sedge/Cyperus vaginatus.

Eastern Banjo Frog, also known as the Bullfrog or Pobblebonk, spends much of the year underground but emerges towards the end of winter/early spring to breed. Tadpoles hatch in about a week and take from 4-15 months to develop into a frog.

Wildlife Index

Selected Bibliography

J Aitchison, The Shark and the Albatross (2015)
T Berkinshaw, Mangroves to Mallee (2009)
Hunt, Grund, Keane & Forrest, Attracting Butterflies to your Garden (2007)
D Lindenmayer et al, Wildlife on Farms (2003)
M Pollan, The Botany of Desire (2002)
S Richards, South Australian Native Bees (2011)
Dr P Rismiller The Echidna, Australia's Enigma (1999)
M J Tyler & S J Walker, Frogs of South Australia (2011)

Photo credits

All credits proceed from top left hand corner photo of the page in a clockwise direction ie a, b, c etc. All other photos by the author.

Guy Draper cover photo b, 1,2b,c,4d,e,6b,d,e,7b,8b,c,9b,10b,c,14a,c,16b,c,22b, 24c,27b, 29a,c,34b,35b,36a,37d,39a,41a,b, 45a, 46b,53c, 58d.

Don Helbig 5a,16e,32b,36c,d, 38a,b,40d,44a,d,47a,50d,54c,56c,57b.

Jeremy Gramp 16a,24a,50c,51c,59b,60d,63d,e.

Mary Retallack 18b,c,25a,c,26 c,d,58b.

Tony & Sheila Sacree 3b,12c,30a,45b,c,61c.

L F Hunt/Butterfly Conservation SA Inc 28c,31b,33a,c,53b,58c.

Dr Mike McKelvey & Dr Peggy Rismiller cover photo d, 43a,b,44c,48d; John Spiers 6c,7c,15c,37c,41c; Steve Walker 44b,46d,62a,b,63c; Simon Slattery cover photo c, back cover photo; Stuart Blackwell 37b,38c,39c; Graham Powell 12b,20b,40c; Andrew Buckle 4c,4d,50a; Roy Baier 51a,b; Jeff Groves 15a,22d; Peter Gower 11b,61b;Trees for Life 32a,c; Frank Gallasch 26b,48c; R H Fisher/SA Museum 20c,49b; Amanda Pearce 40a; Prof Mike Keller/Dr Maryam Yazdani 18d; NRM 61d; Greg Kretschmer 16d; Colin Cock 39b; Rob Wallace 25b; Martin Stokes 56b; Teresa Jack 35a; Sally Pfeiffer 36b; Di Davidson 52a; Sophie Schneider 48a; John Stafford 57a; James Smith/FauNature 48b; Steven Smith 66; Chris Steeles 60c.

Endnotes

Tree Stories
1 p3 V Branson, personal communication
2 p5 I Falkenberg, pers. comm.
3 p5 SA Murray-Darling Basin NRM Board Wedge-tailed Eagles in Agricultural Areas p 4
4 p7 Dr P Horton, pers. comm.
5 p9 H A Ford & D C Paton, The Dynamic Partnership, p 13
6 p15 ed. C R Twidale, M J Tyler & B P Webb Natural History of the Adelaide Region (1976) p24

Bushy Tales: shrubs
1 p17 Dr M Yazdani, pers comm
2 p18 diagram with assistance from Dr M Yazdani and M Retallack
3 p18 M Retallack, pers. comm;
4, 5 p25 ibid.
6 p26 ibid.
7 p27 G&S Kretschmer, pers. comm.
8 p31 J Wormald, song title

Wildlife section
1 p36 J Liersch, pers. comm.
2 p38 Dr P Rismiller, The Echidna, Australias Enigma 1999, pp 99,104
3 p38 G Kretschmer, pers. comm.
4 p39 I Falkenberg, Peregrine Falcon Breeding Site Management & Protection on Public Lands in SA. Aust. Raptor Conference, Raptors in a Changing Landscape, Adelaide Zoo, Aug 2013

5 p39 P D Olsen (1995), Australian Birds of Prey Uni of NSW Press, Sydney Aust.
6 p39 I Falkenberg et al (1991) Organochloride Pesticide contamination in three species of raptors and their prey in SA. Wildlife Research.21: 163-173
7 p41 I Falkenberg, pers. comm
8 p41 P Slater Field Guide to Australian Birds (1983) vol 2 p135
9 p43 Dr P Rismiller The Echidna, Australias Enigma (1999) p100
10 p43 Dr M McKelvey, pers. comm.
11 p45 P Henschke, pers. comm.
12 p44 TS Eliot, The Love Song of J Alfred Prufrock, line 74

Smaller stories
1 p47 A Heuzenroeder Barossa Food, pp149/50
2 p48 D Stammer, pers. comm.
3 p49 D Paton, notes on talk to Mistletoe Action Group, Clare, Feb 2001
4 p55 Dr K Hogendoorn, pers. comm.
5,6 p56 ibid.
7 p57 D Falkenberg, pers. comm.
8 p58 M Retallack, pers. comm.
9 p58 Dr M Yazdani, pers. comm.
10 p60 ed. R C Davis (2002) The Central Australian Expedition 1844-1846, The Journals of Charles Sturt, pp.20, 21, 28, 40, 56, 321
11 p61 B Rice pers. comm.